HOW TO PREPARE FOR THE
NEXT CRYPTO BULL RUN
(2024 BULL RUN)

:Beginners guide to the best coins to
buy and how to maximize your profit

Jack A. Robbins

TABLE OF CONTENT

INTRODUCTION

In 2021, Bitcoin experienced a significant surge, reaching an all-time high of $68,000. This bullish momentum extended to other cryptocurrencies, with Ethereum hitting $4,800, Cardano reaching $2.9, Litecoin soaring to $345, and various tokens achieving their peak values. Bitcoin saw a 2000% increase, while Ethereum and Cardano witnessed pumps of 7000% and 17,000%, respectively. Similar substantial gains were observed in Litecoin, Dogecoin, Solana, and numerous other crypto assets. Those who seized the opportunity during the bull run enjoyed substantial profits.

However, the subsequent correction during the 2022 bear cycle marked the end of the bull run. Now, there's anticipation for the next bull run in the cryptocurrency market.

If you've been on the sidelines during the crypto winter, you might feel a bit out of touch. The fear of missing out (FOMO) can be overwhelming, prompting impulsive decisions to re-enter the market. It's crucial to resist such impulses and instead, develop a well-thought-out plan.

Having a plan in place is essential to avoid hasty decisions and to maximize potential gains during the next bull run.

This guide offers a comprehensive overview of the upcoming crypto bull run. It delves into the factors influencing the next bull run, explores general trends affecting such cycles, and provides insights on how to prepare for it to maximize benefits. Additionally, the guide highlights potential pitfalls that should be avoided to prevent losses even in the midst of a bullish market. Taking a strategic and informed approach will be key to navigating the complexities of the next crypto bull run successfully.

Chapter 1

What Is A Crypto Bull Run?

In the realm of investments, a bull run signifies a period where a majority of investors are actively buying assets. This phase is characterized by a higher demand for assets compared to the available supply, driven by a positive sentiment among investors.

On price charts, the value of a token exhibits a continuous upward trajectory, reflecting the overall bullish outlook of investors toward their investments. This upward movement is indicative of a collective belief that the asset's price will continue to rise.

During a bull run, investors who anticipate price increases take control of the market dynamics. Their optimism and confidence create a positive feedback loop, encouraging other investors to join in and contribute to the buying pressure. As more individuals invest, the overall demand for the asset increases, leading to a subsequent rise in its price.

What Are The Key Indicators Of The Bull Market?

Bull markets are shaped by various factors, but certain elements are consistently observed across most bullish cycles.

These are:

1. Price growth Is Significant

Substantial price growth serves as a primary signal of a bullish market. In a bull cycle, an asset's value experiences prolonged upward movement, evident through recurring green patterns on daily and weekly candle charts. The asset often remains in the overbought zone, with the Relative Strength Index (RSI) consistently above 70, yet without sudden sell-offs.

2. Bitcoin Potential

Bitcoin's role is crucial in a bull market. In the previous bullish phase, Bitcoin displayed a sequence of multiple positive price movements, interrupted by minor declines and followed by substantial upward trends, propelling the overall market higher.

3. High Investor Confidence

Positive investor sentiment is a hallmark of bull cycles. Investors express confidence and optimism in their investments during these periods, often sharing their bullish views on social media platforms. This optimistic outlook is visually represented on price charts by consecutive sequences of large green candles.

4. Cryptocurrency liquidity

Even cryptocurrencies with lower market capitalization, typically perceived as riskier ventures, exhibit substantial price growth. This creates an environment of Fear of Missing Out (FOMO) for crypto assets. To assist in selecting budget-friendly options, we've compiled a list of

Top 15 cryptocurrencies priced under $1 to buy in 2024

1. Bitcoin Minetrix (BTCMTX) – A project with high potential featuring an innovative mining concept.
2. Bitcoin ETF Token (BTC ETF) – An under $1 token inspired by Bitcoin ETF.

3. TG.Casino ($TGC) – A presale casino project gaining popularity below $1.

4. Launchpad XYZ (LPX) – A Web 3 crypto priced under $1, simplifying Web 3.

5. yPredict (YPRED) – An AI-driven cryptocurrency available at an affordable price.

6. Chimpzee (CHMPZ) – A recent eco-friendly project offered under $1.

7. Wall Street Memes (WSM) – The best under $1 memecoin supported by a large community.

8. TRON (TRX) – A cryptocurrency under $1 known for its stability.

9. Enjin (EJN) – An ecosystem and platform catering to individuals, businesses, and developers.

10. Decentraland (MANA) – An opportunity to own virtual land in the metaverse.

11. Cardano (ADA) – Contributing to the sustainability of cryptocurrencies.

12. Ripple (XRP) – A large-cap cryptocurrency available under $1 with great utility.

13. Polygon (MATIC) – Positioned as Ethereum's improved version at a fraction of its price.

14. Cronos (CRO) – An entry into the Crypto.com ecosystem.

15. Stellar (XLM) – A low-cost blockchain designed for cross-border transactions.

5. Lowering Employment Rate

Bull markets establish a profitable environment for corporate entities. The increased financial resources available to individuals during these periods translate into higher consumer spending, resulting in heightened profits for businesses. This positive economic trend empowers organizations to expand their operations, contributing to an increase in employment levels. Consequently, this positive cycle is reflected in a declining unemployment rate as companies hire more personnel to meet the growing demands of a flourishing economy.

6. Positive Economic Indicators

A significant contributing factor to a bull market is a robust economy. In times of economic prosperity, goods and services become more affordable, fostering a favorable environment for financial growth. It is observable on price charts that bull markets often align with positive economic indicators, showcasing a correlation between economic well-being and the upward trends in asset prices. The affordability and overall positive economic conditions during these periods further stimulate investor confidence and participation in the market.

Chapter 2

Cryptocurrencies

Occasionally, indications of a diminishing recession align with bull cycles. Though relatively uncommon, these occurrences do take place. In certain instances, the signs of economic downturns easing coincide with the emergence of bull markets in the financial landscape. This correlation suggests that periods of economic recovery or stabilization may contribute to the initiation or strengthening of bullish trends in various markets.

General Factors That Will Influence The Upcoming Bull Cycle

Assuming you're discussing the next bullish phase, let's explore the factors that could influence it.

Metaverse

The metaverse is undergoing increased interactivity as Web 3.0 gains prominence, driven by a growing awareness of decentralization. Major companies are entering the metaverse, transforming virtual environments into a mainstream phenomenon.

These environments prioritize accessibility and user-friendly search features.

A notable shift is observed as people move away from traditional typing methods to embrace voice-based searches. Forward-thinking businesses are quick to adapt to this shift, implementing interactive communication modes to enhance user experiences. The metaverse is expanding as different virtual worlds seek interconnectedness.

An illustrative example is Bored Ape Yacht Club's (BAYC) Otherside initiative, aiming to unite numerous non-fungible tokens (NFTs) within one virtual world. This endeavor has spurred the development of cross-chain communication, making interoperability more prevalent. With increased versatility backed by this interoperability, the metaverse is poised for significant growth. For more comprehensive insights, refer to our guide on the best metaverse coins to consider for potential success in the upcoming crypto bull cycle.

Artificial intelligence

The artificial intelligence (AI) industry is experiencing a notable surge in growth, currently valued at 100 billion USD. This upswing in interest is further fueled by influential entities such as ChatGPT. According to Statista, projections indicate that the AI market is expected to reach an impressive 2 trillion dollars by the year 2030.

This substantial expansion underscores the increasing significance and widespread adoption of AI technologies across various sectors and industries.

AI Crypto Bull Run

Moreover, the integration of artificial intelligence (AI) into blockchain technology is gaining momentum. This convergence holds the potential to create novel applications across various industries. AI-centric cryptocurrencies are already making strides, exemplified by tokens like Fetch.ai, which employs AI technology to establish a decentralized machine learning network. Another noteworthy project, The Graph, is dedicated to developing a decentralized search engine for users.

With the emergence of multiple AI-driven use cases, their decentralization through blockchain technology is poised to reinforce the upcoming bull cycle. To assist you in navigating this evolving landscape, we've compiled a list of the

Top 10 AI cryptocurrencies for consideration in 2023/2024:

1. yPredict (YPRED) — An AI project offering a predictions marketplace featuring trading signals.
2. Launchpad XYZ (LPX) — A growing AI project designed for traders to capitalize on substantial profits.
3. Meme Kombat (MK) — Enabling users to place bets on AI-generated battles for exciting rewards.

4. Fetch (FET) — A strong-performing AI cryptocurrency, exhibiting noteworthy performance in early 2023.

5. iExec RLC (RLC) — An AI-powered crypto revolutionizing applications in big data, FinTech, and more.

6. Ocean Protocol (OCEAN) — Utilizing AI to unlock and monetize data in a decentralized manner.

7. SingularityNET (AGIX) — Serving as an online AI algorithm marketplace.

8. Velas (VLX) — An AI-powered cryptocurrency with a revolutionary use case.

9. VIDT DAO (VIDT) — An open-source AI crypto token verifying trust within the Web3 ecosystem.

10. Cortex (CTXC) — An AI-powered contract cryptocurrency, offering innovative functionalities.

DeFi

Decentralized finance (DeFi) is gradually gaining traction, partly attributed to the decline of centralized banks such as Signature and Silicon Valley Bank. This shift has prompted traditional financial products to transition into the realm of DeFi. As centralized banking institutions face challenges, decentralized alternatives are emerging as viable and attractive options for users seeking more inclusive, transparent, and autonomous financial solutions. The integration of traditional financial products into the decentralized space represents a notable evolution in the financial landscape, signaling the ongoing transformation and expansion of DeFi platforms.

DeFi liquidity

According to reports, the decentralized finance (DeFi) sector is projected to experience substantial growth at a rate of 42.6% over the next seven years. Innovations like cross-chain interoperability are expected to contribute to the scalability of DeFi, fostering increased adoption.

For those looking to navigate the DeFi landscape in 2023,

here are some of the top DeFi coins:

1. Launchpad XYZ: A new DeFi coin focusing on building a decentralized exchange (DEX) and enhancing trading skills.

2. yPredict: An AI-based DeFi token designed to provide crypto signals and predictions.

3. Maker: A decentralized crypto lending platform.

4. Curve: A decentralized exchange with a specific emphasis on stablecoin trading.

5. Aave: A DeFi platform enabling lending and borrowing of cryptocurrencies.

6. Uniswap: A leading decentralized exchange (DEX) with a range of features for earning through crypto.

7. Compound: A decentralized money market protocol.

8. Sushiswap: The native token of a popular decentralized exchange.

9. DY DX: A decentralized exchange that supports perpetual trading.

10. Synthetix: A decentralized platform specializing in derivatives trading.

11. Loopring: A layer 2 DeFi scaling solution.

Web3 Gaming

The bull cycle of 2021 and the subsequent NFT boom propelled gaming into the spotlight. However, Web3 games have faced some skepticism from long-time gamers who perceive NFTs in games as a "commodification of gameplay." Additionally, these web3 games have been criticized for their minimalistic nature, largely attributed to their exclusive reliance on the Ethereum blockchain.

While the surge in interest in NFTs and blockchain technology has brought new dimensions to the gaming industry, it has also generated discussions and concerns among traditional gamers. The integration of non-fungible tokens (NFTs) into games has been met with criticism, with some gamers expressing reservations about the impact on the intrinsic value and experience of gameplay.

Web3

Positive shifts are occurring in the web3 gaming space. Binance Smart Chain has emerged as the leading choice, covering over 38.11% of new games in this niche. This blockchain introduces flexibility, addressing some of the limitations associated with Ethereum, which is crucial for the development of more advanced and feature-rich games.

Here is a quick list of the best web3 cryptocurrencies to consider for investment in 2023 and beyond:

1. Bitcoin Minetrix: A web3 crypto project revitalizing cloud mining.

2. Bitcoin ETF Token: A top web3 project linked to Bitcoin's growth.

3. Meme Kombat: A brand-new web3 crypto revolutionizing play-to-earn (P2E) gaming.
4. TG.Casino: A web3 crypto casino aiming to elevate online casino experiences.

5. Launchpad XYZ: An emerging crypto project with a web3-propagation concept.

6. yPredict: A new crypto driven by AI, focusing on predictions.

7. Chimpanzee: A top green web3 crypto available in presale in 2023.

8. Wall Street Memes: Recognized as the best meme coin to invest in for 2023.

9. Biconomy: A web3 crypto listed on eToro.

10. API3: Regarded as the best web3 crypto for DeFi infrastructure.

11. Livepeer Recognized as the best web3 cryptocurrency for live streaming.

12. Theta: Acknowledged as the best web3 crypto for video streaming.

13. Polkadot: A leading web3 crypto with a large market cap.

14. Chainlink: Considered the best web3 crypto for smart contract development.

15. Filecoin: Recognized as the best web3 crypto for decentralized storage services.

16. Attention Token: Acknowledged as the best web3 crypto for digital advertising services.

Regulatory Development

The forthcoming bull run in the crypto space is expected to be significantly influenced by regulatory developments. The year 2023 has witnessed substantial advancements in the crypto sector, with countries actively working on crafting crypto laws to regulate the market. Simultaneously, regulatory bodies such as the SEC (U.S. Securities and Exchange Commission) are under increasing pressure to establish clear and comprehensive rules regarding cryptocurrencies.

This regulatory landscape is characterized by a dual approach: on one end, countries are formulating regulations to oversee and govern the crypto market, emphasizing the need for legal frameworks to address the growing industry. On the other end, regulatory bodies like the SEC are grappling with the challenge of defining precise rules and guidelines for the crypto space.

CBDC

The regulatory environment, whether it promotes or hinders, will ultimately shape the performance of the crypto market during a bull cycle. Progressive regulations providing clarity and fostering innovation tend to boost market sentiment,

while unclear or restrictive regulations can introduce uncertainty, impacting investor confidence and market growth. In essence, regulatory factors play a crucial role in determining the success and dynamics of a crypto bull cycle.

When Is The Next Bull Run Coming

Predicting the timing of the next bull run in the crypto market is inherently speculative, given the ever-changing nature of market dynamics. However, historically, crypto bull runs have often coincided with Bitcoin Halving events.

Bitcoin Halving occurs approximately every four years and involves a reduction in block rewards by half. In the upcoming halving expected in 2024, when the number of block hits reaches 740k, the block rewards will decrease from 6.25 to 3.125 Bitcoins. This reduction in the rate of new Bitcoin issuance is a significant event in the cryptocurrency market, and its historical association with bull runs has led many to closely monitor Bitcoin Halving as a potential catalyst for the next bullish cycle. To find the exact timing of the next Bitcoin halving, you can refer to our detailed guide.

Chapter 3

Bitcoin Next Halving

With only 21 million Bitcoin tokens in existence, the Bitcoin halving event serves to enhance the scarcity of BTC by reducing the block rewards. Historically, this scarcity-driven mechanism has been associated with initiating bull runs in the price of Bitcoin.

Notably, Changpeng Zhao, a prominent figure in the crypto space, has recently predicted that the next bull cycle will unfold approximately a year after the next halving event. This anticipation aligns with the expectation that reduced supply, coupled with sustained demand, can contribute to the upward momentum of Bitcoin's price in the post-halving period.

How To Prepare For The Next Bull Cycle?

Below are 5 tips to help you prepare for the next bull run:

1. How to React, and Not Predict:

- Every crypto cycle is unique, and historical data, while useful, may not provide a complete picture of future trends.

- The crypto market is highly volatile, with diverse opinions and strong supporters.

Stay flexible and be open to reacting to market changes with discipline.

List of Most Volatile Cryptocurrencies of 2023 and beyond

- Bitcoin Minetrix: Overall Most Volatile Crypto of 2023

- Bitcoin Token ETF: The Volatile Crypto of 2023 Following The Development of Bitcoin ETFs

- Meme Kombat: The Volatile Crypto of 2023 in the Memecoin Niche

- TG.Casino: The Volatile Crypto Powering a Telegram Crypto Casino

- Launchpad XYZ: Web 3 Crypto to Increase Web 3 Adoption Rate
- yPredict: A Crypto Helping Users Navigate the Volatile Crypto Market

- Chimpzee: The Green Crypto that Rewards Users for Trading

- Wall Street Memes: A Potential To Become the Most Volatile Crypto of 2023

- Tamadoge: A Pumped 20x on OKX exchange on launch

- Bitcoin: The Frontrunner cryptocurrency with high volatility on low timeframes

- Dogecoin: Top grossing volatile memecoin

- Terra Classic: Most volatile cryptocurrency of the past year

- Binance Coin: The High volatility token powering the biggest crypto exchange

- Shiba Inu: A Volatile meme cryptocurrency with a huge community

- Solana: A Strong fundamental project set for volatile bounce in 2023

2. Selling Extra Assets To Raise Cash Levels:

- Ensure ample buying power to navigate market shifts by selling extra assets.
- Avoid emotional attachment and promptly liquidate assets lacking potential to maintain capital and increase cash reserves.

3. Participating In Crypto Presales:

- Engage in crypto presales, particularly those with utilities like Bitcoin ETF Token and Bitcoin Minetrix, offering significant upside potential upon listing.

4. Bitcoin Minetrix:

Tokens adhering to their roadmap during retraces can regain momentum and become sustainable long-term assets.

Bitcoin ETF Token and Bitcoin Minetrix, as utility cryptos, show potential for exponential growth if they stay true to their long-term goals.

Analysts, like Jacob Bury, express confidence in the potential of Bitcoin ETF Token, predicting 10x returns for early investors.

11 Cryptocurrencies With Most Potential Buy In 2023/2024

Here's a concise list of the most profitable cryptocurrencies to consider buying in 2023:

- Bitcoin Minetrix: A stake-to-mine utility token with significant potential.
- Bitcoin ETF Token: A crypto asset closely tied to the development of Bitcoin ETFs.
- Meme Kombat: An AI-driven battle arena featuring meme avatars.
- TG.Casino: A crypto casino on Telegram with notable upsides.

- Wall Street Memes: A promising new meme coin with a substantial community of supporters.
- yPredict: A highly promising crypto project offering solutions to enhance trading.
- Launchpad XYZ: A crypto project facilitating easier adoption of Web3.
- Quant: A popular crypto project specializing in blockchain interoperability.
- Solana: A highly scalable network.
- Ethereum: The second-largest cryptocurrency and the largest smart contract-based blockchain platform.

- Bitcoin: The largest cryptocurrency by market capitalization.

5. Buying during crash

Active traders can capitalize on short-term trading opportunities during bear markets, where sudden and substantial surges, such as Pepe Coin's 83,000% increase within 10 days, create favorable conditions for quick trades. While awaiting the next bull cycle, focusing on short-term trades and identifying the best cryptocurrencies to buy during market downturns is crucial.

Best Cryptos to Buy During the Crash:

- Bitcoin Minetrix: The Overall Best Crypto to Buy During the Crash.
- Bitcoin ETF Token: Bitcoin ETF-Inspired Token Recommended Amidst a Crash.
- Meme Kombat: GameFi Project with Betting Elements, Providing Opportunities During a Crash.
- TG.Casino: Top Crypto Casino with High Potential, Especially During Market Declines.
- Launchpad XYZ: An All-in-One Crypto for Web3 Products, Considered a Good Investment During a Crash.

- yPredict: An AI Crypto with AI-Driven Trading Signals to Navigate the Market.
- Chimpzee: Best Green Crypto to Buy During a Crash.
- Wall Street Memes: Top Memecoin Recommended for Purchase During Market Downturns.
- Litecoin: Best Alternative to Bitcoin, Suggested for Purchase During Crypto Crashes.
- Quant: DeFi Project Aiming to Build Interoperability Between Multiple Blockchains.
- Chainlink: Popular DeFi Platform Supporting Secure Interaction Between Blockchains and External Data.

- Ethereum: The Second Largest Cryptocurrency and a Well-Established Crypto Project.
- Basic Attention Token: Popular Token Designed to Enhance Transparency in Marketing.
- Solana: The Ethereum Competitor Providing Faster and Secure Transactions on Blockchain.

6. Researching and select Tokens

In a bear market, it is opportune to retain existing tokens and explore new investment opportunities. Dedicate time to researching the various crypto assets in the market, identifying those with the highest potential for growth.

This proactive approach allows investors to stay informed and strategically position themselves for potential gains as market conditions evolve.

7. How to Create An Investment Plan

Cryptocurrency, known for its erratic nature, demands a careful and methodical approach rather than impulsive decisions during market upswings. Here's a recommended strategy:

- Develop an Investment Plan: Instead of hastily investing, craft a comprehensive investment plan or thesis to guide the allocation of funds across different crypto assets.

- Thoughtful Fund Allocation: Determine the amount you're comfortable investing in established cryptocurrencies like Bitcoin and Ethereum. Simultaneously, decide on the allocation for alternative coins (altcoins).
- Diversify Across Industries: When selecting altcoins, assess industries with growth potential and distribute your portfolio accordingly. For example, allocate percentages to areas like artificial intelligence (AI), real-world assets, and Layer-2 solutions.
- Implement Dollar-Cost Averaging: To navigate market fluctuations effectively, consider adopting a

dollar-cost averaging strategy. This involves systematically investing a fixed amount at regular intervals, allowing you to benefit from market dips by acquiring assets at varying prices.

8. How to Set Profit Target And Stick To Them

One of the most significant pitfalls in investing is the failure to determine the opportune moment to secure profits. This challenge is particularly pronounced in the realm of cryptocurrency, where market dynamics are heavily influenced by emotions, social media trends, sudden sensations, and, frankly, avarice.

During periods of price escalation, it's crucial to establish realistic profit-taking targets and adhere to them diligently. A disciplined approach to profit-taking serves as a safeguard against abrupt market downturns.

If uncertainties surround your exit strategy, consider a phased approach by employing a dollar-cost averaging strategy for selling. For example, divest 25% of an altcoin at a designated price point, another 25% at a subsequent price point, and so forth.

9. How to Diversify Your Risk

While Bitcoin and Ethereum are considered stalwart cryptocurrencies, investors often turn to altcoins for their potential for higher risk and reward.

Given the increased risk associated with altcoins, it's prudent to allocate only a small portion of your portfolio to them. Although the potential for rewards is higher, this approach prevents overexposure to risk and safeguards against excessive downside.

It's crucial to recognize that gains in the altcoin market can be fleeting, and many altcoins are not well-suited for long-term buy-and-hold strategies.

Substantial declines, often exceeding 95%, are not uncommon between market cycles and downturns.

10. Research-based decision making

Avoid succumbing to investment decisions driven by hype or the fear of missing out (FOMO).

Cryptocurrency stands out as an asset class due to the transparent nature of its transactions, all of which are recorded on a public blockchain for scrutiny. Harnessing the wealth of tools and information available can empower you to make informed decisions, eliminating the need to rely on ambiguous indicators as seen in other markets.

Here are some free tools that can enhance your analytical toolkit:

1. ai: Input any address to receive a detailed breakdown of its portfolio, transactions, and more.
Gain comprehensive insights into individual blockchains, decentralized applications (dApps), layer-2 solutions, and decentralized finance (DeFi) with metrics such as Total Value Locked and trade volume.

2. Fi: Functions as an "anti-virus scanner" for cryptocurrencies and smart contracts, designed to identify intentional rug-pulls and detect malicious or flawed smart contract code.

3. Arkham Intelligence: A blockchain visualizer enabling a clear

understanding of the relationships between wallets. Use it to flag suspicious transfers or prevent errors in airdrop farming.

4. Crypto-fundraising.info: Tracks venture capital funding for new crypto projects, providing insights into the amount raised and the contributing firms.

Leverage these tools for in-depth research into a project's fundamentals, team composition, and market standing. Conducting a SWOT analysis will aid in identifying strengths and weaknesses within a project.

11. Risk Management

Risk management is a crucial aspect that new traders must prioritize, yet it is frequently neglected until it becomes problematic. To effectively manage risk, start by determining the amount you can comfortably risk on your overall investment and steadfastly adhere to that limit.

Additionally, calculate the maximum you can afford to lose on any single trade and enforce this by employing a stop-loss order to cap losses in case the market turns unfavorable. Reinforce these risk management strategies by steering clear of emotional decision-making and formulate an investment plan that outlines target entry and exit prices.

While staying informed about news and market developments is essential, it's advisable to restrict exposure to social media, which often contains exaggerated information and can tempt you into making overly ambitious decisions.

12. Noteworthy Cryptocurrencies

It's essential to conduct a thorough analysis of price charts while also delving into the underlying technology and adoption rate of any cryptocurrency. For instance, in the growing field of artificial intelligence, a crypto driven by AI is likely to capture the community's attention, particularly during bullish market trends. A similar scenario can unfold for DeFi tokens. Compile a list of these assets, monitor their performance, and seize the opportunity to purchase them when they reach early bear market lows in anticipation of the upcoming bull season.

Quick Guide on How to Purchase Cryptocurrency

If you're eager to buy cryptocurrencies like Bitcoin promptly, you can follow these four rapid steps to kickstart your journey.

- Open an Account: Begin by opening an account with a reputable cryptocurrency broker. We recommend eToro.com due to its robust regulation, support for multiple deposit options, and inclusion of copy trading features.

- Upload ID: Since eToro is a regulated brokerage platform, you'll be required to upload a copy of your government-issued ID.
- Deposit: Fund your account by depositing funds through options such as debit/credit cards, Paypal, Neteller, Skrill, or bank wire.
- Buy Cryptocurrency: Locate your preferred cryptocurrency and click on the 'Trade' button to initiate the purchase.

Mistakes To Avoid During Bull Runs

1. Being Greedy

A bull market is not everlasting; it eventually concludes. Therefore, exercising caution is essential. Be selective in identifying opportunities. If you observe a surge in an asset's price that pushes it into the overbought zone, recognize that it is overpriced and likely to undergo a correction. Some individual investors disregard this signal, leading them to bear losses at the peak of the bull market. Avoid excessive optimism driven by greed and prioritize thorough research before making investment decisions.

2. Switching Your Investment Process Drastically

Bull markets can create a deceptive feeling of security. The prolonged upward trend in financial markets, marked by consistent gains, lures inexperienced traders into altering their risk portfolios significantly, even if they were previously risk-averse.

3. Bitcoin Bull

Traders often abandon their proven strategies to invest in assets that are excessively hyped by the media. While there's nothing inherently problematic with considering influencers' opinions, it's crucial to recognize that not everyone provides reliable advice.

Yielding to misguided influences can lead to financial losses. However, for trustworthy trading insights, you may consider following recommended cryptocurrency YouTube channels.

News

Crypto Guides

Gaming

Trading

PRSearch Inside Bitcoins

20 Best Crypto Youtube Channels to learn from

- Jacob Crypto Bury
- Rekt Capital
- Coin Bureau
- Altcoin Daily
- Ivan on Tech
- DataDash

- Crypto Jebb
- Crypto Zombie
- The Modern Investor
- BitBoy Crypto
- Crypto Daily
- Crypto Banter
- Chico Crypto
- Nugget's News
- Crypto Tips
- Hashashi
- Digital Asset News
- Benjamin Cowen
- Boxmining
- Crypto

These channels offer extensive information on a wide range of topics, spanning from Bitcoin and Ethereum to the latest developments in DeFi projects and NFTs.

Whether you're an experienced investor seeking valuable market insights or a newcomer aiming to understand the fundamentals of blockchain technology, these channels cater to diverse interests within the cryptocurrency space.

4. Using The Wrong Exchange

Be cautious when dealing with new exchanges that may charge high fees, often citing their novelty as a justification. Resist the allure and recognize that elevated fees can diminish your profit margins. Opt for exchanges like OKX, Binance, Bybit, and eToro, which offer a low-fee model without compromising on diverse trading opportunities.

While analyzing crypto trading charts is beneficial for understanding trends, relying solely on technical indicators may be insufficient. Cryptocurrency prices can exhibit unexpected patterns, as seen in the recent surge in namecoin. Therefore, it's essential to supplement technical analysis with a broader perspective.

To maximize your market insights, consider incorporating social indicators. Stay updated on news and social media posts, as they can provide valuable insights into an asset's performance based on its developments. Don't solely depend on charts;

a well-rounded approach includes staying informed about the broader context through news and social media.

Chapter 4

How To Find The End Of Bull Runs?

Bull runs can extend over months or even years, presenting lucrative investment opportunities. However, it's crucial to recognize that these bullish trends are not perpetual, and investing at the wrong time can result in holding assets at their peak value. Determining the conclusion of a bull run is a challenging task.

Bull markets are characterized by non-linear trajectories, often marked by periodic price fluctuations. It's common to observe brief declines, represented by small red candles, amidst a series of consecutive large green candles. These intermittent downturns can be misleading and may be mistakenly interpreted as the end of the bull run.

BTC Bull

Indeed, studying historical charts provides valuable insights into identifying the conclusion of a bull run. Typically, the end of a bull market is characterized by a sharp decline in prices. Analyzing past trends reveals a pattern where a series of small consecutive red candles precedes a significant drop.

This decline signifies the initiation of sell pressure in the market.

The initial appearance of a few red candles creates a ripple effect, setting the stage for a broader shift toward a bear market. Recognizing this pattern is essential for investors seeking to navigate the transitions between bull and bear markets effectively.

FAQs

Which crypto should I buy during a bull run?

Selecting a cryptocurrency during a bull run is contingent on evaluating the asset's current development and future potential. Conduct thorough research, compile a list of cryptocurrencies with upward potential, and analyze their historical trading charts. Assess whether these new cryptocurrencies are adopting upcoming technologies. These guidelines serve as a foundation for identifying promising cryptocurrencies poised for growth during a bull run.

How do you know if crypto is bullish?

Observing a rapid upward trend in a token's price suggests that there is a higher demand from buyers compared to sellers. This trend often indicates that investors are optimistic about the asset's potential for further upward movement. The increase in buying activity reflects a positive sentiment in the market, as more participants are eager to acquire the token, anticipating continued price appreciation.

How long do bull runs last?

The duration of bull runs in the cryptocurrency market is influenced by market conditions.

Some crypto assets have experienced extended bull runs lasting 180-200 days, while others have seen shorter runs lasting only a month. The duration is shaped by a combination of people's perceptions and the fundamental factors influencing the token's market. Factors such as investor sentiment, adoption trends, technological developments, and overall market dynamics play a crucial role in determining the longevity of a bull run.

CONCLUSION

Many believe the next crypto bull run will occur within a year after halving, but its duration and magnitude depend on technological advancements and regulatory changes. Preparation is crucial, emphasizing patience and caution to avoid substantial losses. Prioritize utility-based tokens, employ a comprehensive analysis combining price charts and social media monitoring, and stay well-informed for a potentially profitable next bull run. Consider investments in utility-based tokens like Bitcoin ETF Token.